Introducing Landforms

Bobbie Kalman and Kelley MacAulay

Crabtree Publishing
crabtreebooks.com

Created by Bobbie Kalman

For my cousin Heather Brissenden, with oodles of love.
You are the star of our family!

Crabtree Publishing

crabtreebooks.com   800-387-7650

In Canada: We acknowledge the financial support of the Government of Canada through the Canada Book Fund for our publishing activities.

Editor-in-Chief: Bobbie Kalman
Writing team: Bobbie Kalman, Kelley MacAulay
Editor: Robin Johnson
Copy editor: Michael Hodge
Photo research: Bobbie Kalman, Crystal Sikkens
Design: Katherine Kantor, Samantha Crabtree (cover)
Production manager: Candice Campbell

Hardcover 978-0-7787-3203-7
Paperback 978-0-7787-3213-6

Printed in the U.S.A./CP072026

Library and Archives Canada Cataloguing in Publication
Kalman, Bobbie, 1947-
Introducing landforms / Bobbie Kalman & Kelley MacAulay.
(Looking at earth)
Includes index.
ISBN 978-0-7787-3203-7 (bound).--ISBN 978-0-7787-3213-6 (pbk.)

III. Series.
1. Landforms--Juvenile literature. I. MacAulay, Kelley II. Title.
GB402.K34 2008   j551.41   C2008-900927-4

Published in Canada
Crabtree Publishing
616 Welland Avenue
St. Catharines, Ontario
L2M 5V6

Published in the United States
Crabtree Publishing
347 Fifth Avenue
Suite 1402-145
New York, NY 10016

Illustrations:
Barbara Bedell: page 13 (green and white fish)
Katherine Kantor: pages 4, 13 (blue fish), 20
Jeannette McNaughton-Julich: page 14
Bonna Rouse: page 19
Margaret Amy Salter: page 13 (yellow fish)

Photographs:
© iStockphoto.com: pages 5 (middle right), 30 (top left)
© Shutterstock.com: cover, pages 1, 3, 4, 5 (top and bottom right), 6, 7 (top left and right), 8, 9, 10 (bottom), 11, 12, 13, 14, 15, 16, 17 (except inset), 18, 19, 20, 21, 22, 23, 24, 25, 26, 27, 28, 29 (except bottom left), 30, 31
Other images by Digital Stock, Digital Vision, and Photodisc

Library of Congress Cataloging-in-Publication Data
Kalman, Bobbie.
Introducing landforms / Bobbie Kalman and Kelley MacAulay.
p. cm. -- (Looking at earth)
Includes index.
ISBN-13: 978-0-7787-3203-7 (rlb)
ISBN-10: 0-7787-3203-7 (rlb)
ISBN-13: 978-0-7787-3213-6 (pb)
ISBN-10: 0-7787-3213-4 (pb)
1. andforms--Juvenile literature. 2. Earth sciences--Juvenile literature. I. MacAulay, Kelley. II. Title.
GB406.K26 2008
551.41--dc22

2008004846

Contents

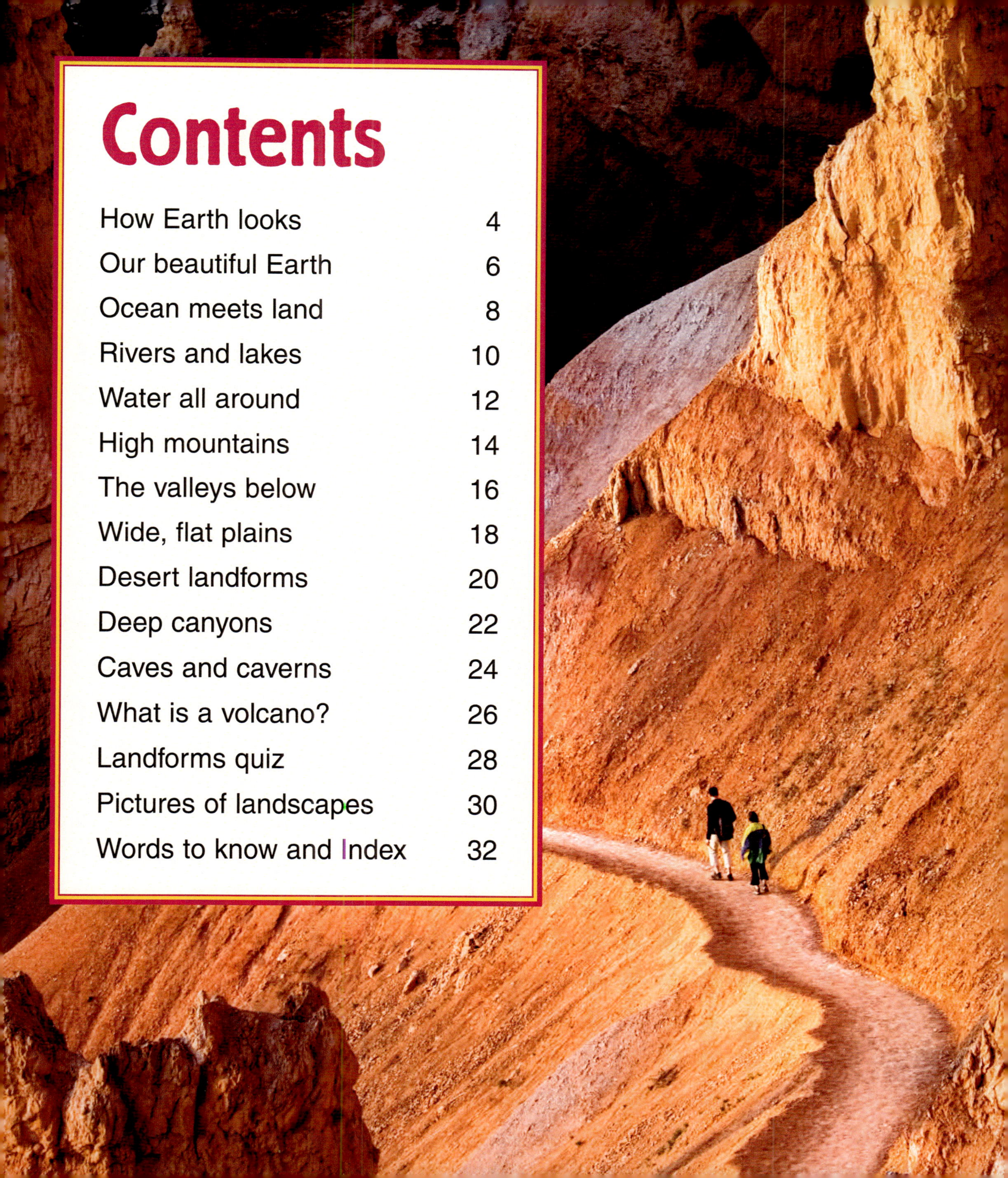

How Earth looks

There are seven huge areas of land on Earth. The areas of land are called **continents**. The continents are North America, South America, Europe, Asia, Africa, Australia and Oceania, and Antarctica. There are huge areas of water around the continents. The areas of water are called **oceans**.

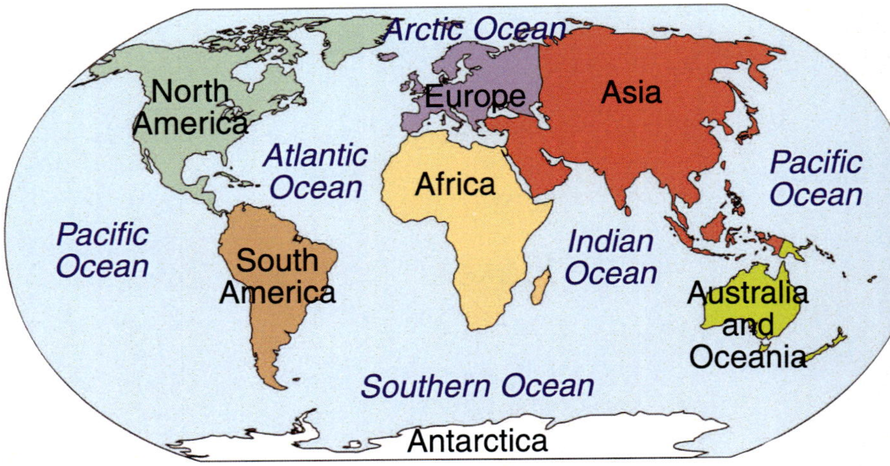

These children are making a map of the continents. Name the continent that each child is painting. Look at the map above if you need help. Which continent is missing from the children's map?

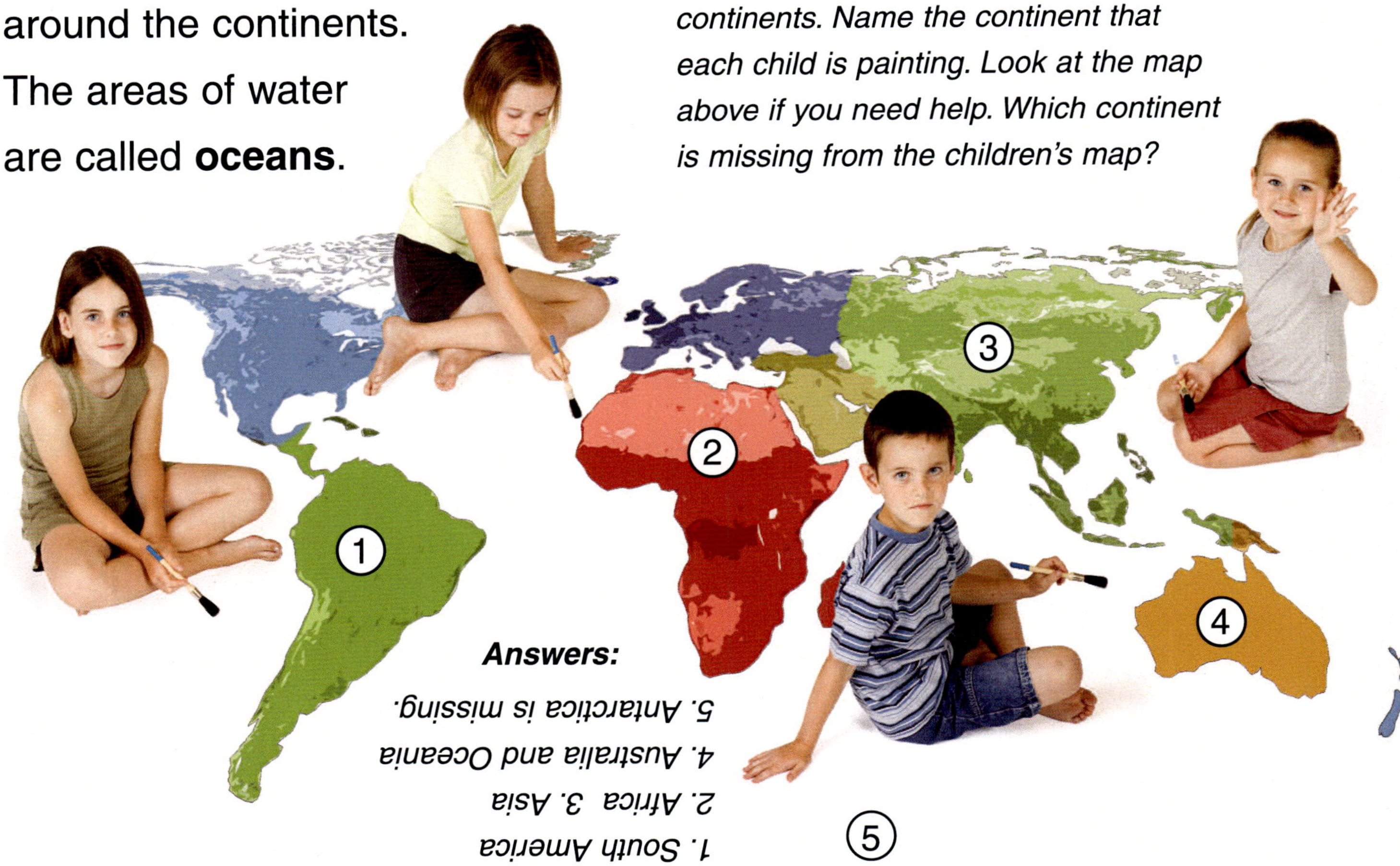

Answers:

1. South America
2. Africa 3. Asia
4. Australia and Oceania
5. Antarctica is missing.

What are landforms?

The continents are Earth's biggest **landforms**. Landforms are different shapes of land on Earth. In some places, the land is flat. In other places, the land is tall and steep. There are many kinds of landforms on Earth.

*Small underwater animals created this **island**.*

What shapes the land?

Landforms are shaped by wind, fire, water, and ice. Landforms are also shaped by movements of the Earth under the ground. Some landforms are shaped by animals or people.

*People created these **peninsulas**.*

Wind and water shape rocks.

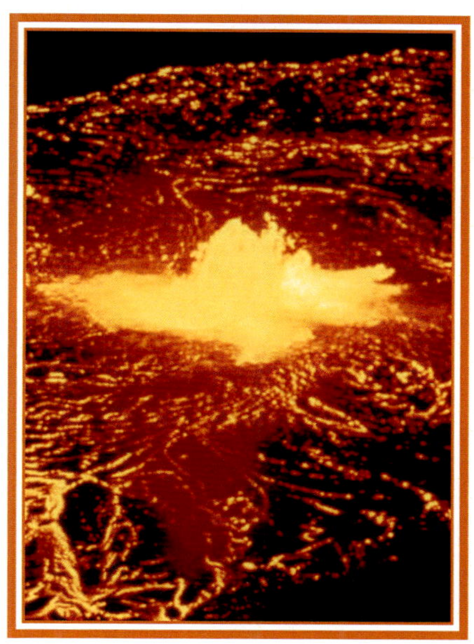

*Fire shapes some **mountains**.*

Ice creates many landforms.

Our beautiful Earth

Landforms are different in different places. They make Earth interesting and beautiful. Without landforms, Earth would look the same everywhere. Look at the pictures on these pages. Are there landforms like these where you live?

*These children are playing on a sandy **beach**. (See page 8.)*

*These people are sliding down a **waterfall** in a **canyon**. (See pages 10 and 22.)*

There are **hills** near this girl's home. She loves sliding down the hills in winter. (See page 14.)

This boy lives near a **coast**. He is exploring a **sea cave**. (See page 9.)

These children are visiting a **desert**. They are learning about **mesas** and **buttes**. (See page 21.) You will learn about these landforms and many more in this book. Keep reading!

Ocean meets land

A coast is a landform. It is the edge of land where it meets an ocean. Coasts can be very different. Some are rocky with **cliffs**. A cliff is a tall, steep rock. Other coasts have beaches. A beach is an area of sand or **pebbles** next to water. The water at many beaches is shallow and clear.

*The water in oceans is **salt water**. Salt water has a lot of salt in it. This girl is playing in shallow ocean water on a beach.*

This rocky coast has tall cliffs.

The coast and water

Peninsulas and sea caves are landforms that are parts of some coasts. Some coasts give the ocean waters near them different shapes. **Bays**, **coves**, and **harbors** are ocean waters that are shaped by coasts. They are shown below.

A sea cave is a large hole in the side of a cliff. The cave is made by waves that hit the cliff many times.

1. A peninsula is land that has water around three sides.
2. A bay is water that has land almost all around it.
3. A cove is a small bay.
4. A harbor is an area of water near a coast where boats are protected from the wind and waves.

Rivers and lakes

Rivers and **lakes** are bodies of water that are on continents. A river is a large stream of water that flows into a lake or an ocean. A lake is a body of water that has land all around it. The water in rivers and lakes is **fresh water**. Fresh water does not have very much salt in it.

Some rivers have waterfalls. The falling water in waterfalls moves very fast!

Most rivers start high up on mountains and flow downhill. Some rivers crash over cliffs in waterfalls. As the rivers flow, they carry rocks and dirt with them. Over time, rivers wear away the land. Rivers can even cut through mountains! In this way, rivers help shape the land on Earth.

What makes lakes?

Lakes form in large **basins** in the Earth. A basin is like a bowl. Many lakes form from melting **glaciers**. A glacier is a slow-moving river of ice. The water in lakes comes mainly from the rivers and streams that flow into them. Some of the water comes from rain and melting snow.

When glaciers melt, the water flows down mountains in rivers. Some of the rivers empty into lakes.

Water all around

Islands are landforms that have water all around them. They are found in oceans, rivers, and lakes. Some islands are huge. Other islands are tiny. This small island is in a lake.

Islands from corals

Some islands are formed from **coral reefs**. Coral reefs are huge underwater landforms found near coasts. They are made up of **corals**. Corals are the hard **skeletons**, or coverings, of tiny animals called **coral polyps**. When coral polyps die, their skeletons are left behind. Coral reefs are made up of the skeletons that pile up. When they pile up above water, islands are formed.

New corals are always growing in coral reefs. When they die, the reefs get bigger.

This island was formed from a coral reef. You can see corals under the water.

There are coral reefs all around this small island. The reefs are under the water.

High mountains

Have you ever climbed a mountain? A mountain is a very high area of rocky land. It is wide at the bottom and narrow at the top. It has steep sides. Mountains that are small and not steep are called hills.

This girl has climbed a mountain. The mountain is rocky and steep. How did she get up there?

Alone or in groups?

Some mountains stand alone. A mountain that stands alone does not have other mountains around it. Most mountains are in groups. A group of mountains is called a **mountain range**. There are many mountain ranges on Earth.

(right) Mount Fuji is a mountain in Japan. There are no other mountains around it.

The weather is cold high on mountains. Few plants and animals live there.

Some mountain ranges are very long. The Rocky Mountain range stretches from British Columbia, Canada, to New Mexico in the United States.

The valleys below

Valleys are low landforms that are between mountains. They are also below mountains. Some valleys have curved sides. Valleys with curved sides are U-shaped. Other valleys have steep sides. Valleys with steep sides are V-shaped. This picture shows a V-shaped valley.

Down in the valley

The weather is warmer in valleys than on the mountains around them. Trees, grasses, and flowers grow in valleys. There are rivers, too. Elk, rabbits, chipmunks, and hawks live in valleys. This horse has found food to eat in a valley.

These elk find food and water in this valley river.

Wide, flat plains

Much of the land on Earth is made up of **plains**. Plains are huge areas of nearly flat land. Some plains are covered in bushes or **forests**. Forests are areas with many trees. Other plains are covered in grasses and flowers. They are called **grasslands** or **prairies**.

There are grasses and many flowers growing on this grassland.

These deer live on a plain with a forest. They are drinking from a river that flows through the plain.

Rabbits live in grasses on plains. These rabbits are hiding in the long grass.

Good for farming

The soil on plains is good for growing **crops**. Crops are plants that people grow for food. Plains are also good places to raise farm animals. On plains, there is plenty of grass to eat for cows, horses, and sheep.

*These sheep are **grazing**, or eating grass, on a plain. Cows and horses also graze on plains.*

Desert landforms

Deserts are dry areas that get very little rain. Strong winds blow in deserts. The winds push sand into huge piles called **dunes**. Dunes are desert landforms.

Desert oasis

In some parts of deserts, there is water under the ground. When the water comes up from the ground, it makes an **oasis**. An oasis is an area in a desert where plants grow.

These palms are growing in a desert oasis.

Mesas and buttes

Mesas are other desert landforms. Mesas are hills and mountains with flat tops and very steep sides. Wind blows sand against the sides of mesas. Over time, the mesas become very narrow. When they become narrow, the mesas are called buttes.

Mesas have flat tops and steep sides.

These buttes are called the "Three Sisters."

Deep canyons

Canyons are landforms that are also found in dry areas. Canyons are much deeper than the land around them is. Many canyons have rivers running through them. The rivers wear away the rocks in the canyons. Over time, the rivers change the shapes of the canyons.

The Colorado River flows through the Grand Canyon. The Grand Canyon is a huge, wide canyon.

Some canyons are very narrow. This girl can touch both sides of this narrow canyon.

Strange shapes

Some canyons have **hoodoos**. Hoodoos are thin rocks that rise up from the ground in dry areas. They have interesting shapes. Some hoodoos look like giant mushrooms. Other hoodoos look like weird creatures.

Many of the hoodoos in Alberta, Canada, look like giant mushrooms.

These hoodoos are in Goblin Valley, Utah. What are ***goblins****?*

There are more hoodoos in Bryce Canyon, Utah, than in any other place on Earth. The hoodoos were formed by wind, water, and ice. People see many shapes in the hoodoos. What do you see?

Caves and caverns

Caves are underground landforms. They are empty areas inside Earth. Some caves have huge rooms. The rooms are called **caverns**. Some caverns are joined by tunnels. There are tunnels deep inside this cavern.

Many caves also have lakes or rivers inside them. There is a small lake inside this cavern.

Stalactites and stalagmites look like icicles. They are formed from minerals in water that have built up into hard rock formations.

Rock formations

Many caves have **rock formations** that are still growing and forming. The formations in caves are made from **minerals**. Some formations hang from the ceilings in caves. They are called **stalactites**. Other formations grow from the ground up. They are called **stalagmites**. Stalactites and stalagmites often join together. When they join together, they are called **columns**.

The stalagmites and stalactites in this cave have joined together and become columns.

Many bats live inside caves. They fly out of the caves at night to find food.

What is a volcano?

A **volcano** is an opening in the Earth's surface. Some volcanoes are **active**, and some are **dormant**, or not active. An active volcano still **erupts**, or explodes. Smoke, ash, and **lava** shoot out from its opening. Lava is hot liquid rock. After lava pours out, it dries and gets hard. Each time a volcano erupts, the dried lava builds up. The volcano gets bigger and bigger.

This volcano is erupting. Hot lava is pouring down the sides of the volcano.

Mountains of lava

Dried lava can get so tall that it makes a mountain! Some volcanoes erupt every day, and the mountains keep growing. Volcanoes that erupt under water become mountains, too. They grow until their tops reach above the surface of water. Their tops become islands.

These mountains formed from dried lava.

Wizard Island is a volcano that formed in the water. It is found in a lake in Oregon.

Landforms quiz

Take this quiz to see how much you have learned about landforms. Match the correct picture to each of these clues. The answers are on the next page.

Which landform...

1. shoots out hot melted rock?
2. has water at its edge and can be rocky or sandy?
3. was made from dead ocean animals called coral polyps?
4. is a large underground room?
5. is deeper than the land around it?
6. has sand or pebbles covered by shallow water?
7. has water on three sides?
8. is taller than a hill?
9. is mainly flat land?
10. is a rock with a weird shape?

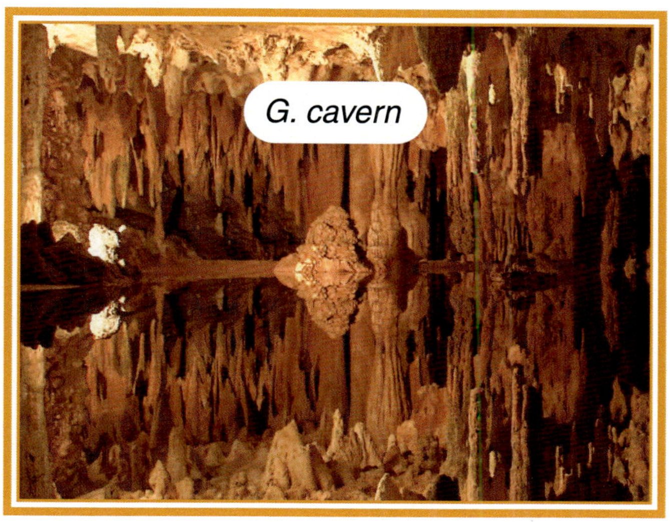

Answers: 1-J; 2-D; 3-E; 4-G; 5-F;
6-B; 7-C; 8-I; 9-H; 10-A

Pictures of landscapes

Are you an artist? Many artists paint **landscapes**. A landscape is how land looks. A landscape may have several kinds of landforms. Paint a landscape that shows some of the landforms you have read about in this book. Have fun!

This young painter's landscape has a lake, a river, and some mountains. Name four colors that she used to paint her landscape.

Which landforms are part of this landscape?

If you prefer, you can take photographs of landscapes. Find landscapes with two or more landforms. The picture below has several landforms. Look for interesting shapes and colors in the landscapes. Once you have taken the photos, you can use them to paint landscapes. Hang up your photos or paintings and enjoy looking at the beauty of our Earth!

Words to know

Note: Some boldfaced words are defined where they appear in the book.

beach A stretch of sand or pebbles that meets a body of water

butte A tall, narrow hill with a flat top and steep sides

canyon A deep valley with steep sides

cliff A tall, steep rock at a coast

coast Land that is beside an ocean

desert A dry area of land where few plants grow

goblin A small, ugly imaginary creature

hill A raised area of land with sloping sides

island An area of land with water all around it

mesa A wide hill or mountain with a flat top and steep, flat sides

mineral A solid non-living substance found in nature that helps plants and animals grow

mountain A very high area of rocky land with steep sides

pebble A small, smooth stone

peninsula An area of land with water around three sides

rock formation A rock with an unusual shape

sea cave A large hole in the side of a cliff beside an ocean

waterfall A place where a river falls over a steep cliff

Index